The Art of Making
Teddy Bears

For Barbara,

Happy bear making!

Best wishes,

Jennifer Laing

2003

MILNER CRAFT SERIES

The Art of Making
Teddy Bears

JENNIFER LAING

SALLY MILNER PUBLISHING

First published in 1993 by
Sally Milner Publishing Pty Ltd
558 Darling Street
Rozelle NSW 2039
Australia

Reprinted 1993

© Jennifer Laing, 1993

Illustrations by Jennifer Laing
Photography by Phillip Castleton
Design concept by Gatya Kelly, Doric Order
Typeset by Asset Typesetting Pty Ltd, Sydney
Printed and bound in Australia by Impact Printing

National Library of Australia Cataloguing-in-Publication entry:

Laing, Jennifer.
   The art of making teddy bears.

   Bibliography.
   Includes index.
   ISBN 1 86351 099 0.

   1. Teddy bears. 2. Soft toy making. I. Title.
   (Series: Milner craft series).

745.5924

DEDICATION

To all my friends in the bear world,
both human and furry.

CONTENTS

THANK YOU

To my family, who have always supported and encouraged me in whatever unusual projects I have been interested.

To Elizabeth and Phillip Castleton, who brought me out of the bear-lovers' closet and let me play in their wonderful bear shop.

To helpful friends with their wonderful collections, especially David Worland and Julie Townsend.

To the Houghton Library of Harvard University for permission to use Clifford Berryman's cartoon.

A special thank you to Sally Milner for making this possible.

INTRODUCTION

Teddy bears mean so many things to so many people. They have only been with us for about ninety years, but they are firmly ensconced in our lives, and in our subconciousness. They seem to have always been there. Teddy bears are one of the few toys that aren't left behind in childhood. Their furry little bodies are so full of love, comfort and affection that they remain a symbol of security to many of us even when we are adults.

Recently, I spent two lovely years managing Australia's first and largest all-bear shop. Initially I thought I would be selling teddy bears for children, but I was wrong. Although there were many proud new parents and grandparents who came to buy the right bear for their new baby to grow up with, the majority of bears were bought for other adults or for the purchasers themselves.

In my time at the Teddy Bear Shop I heard many wonderful and sad tales. People would often come in and confide to me that they still had their old bear, or that he was now taking care of the next generation of their family. Sometimes I would be handed a sad love-worn bear for repairs. Frequently I would be told tragic little stories of how Mum had thrown out their much-loved, though filthy, bear; an act which had left lifelong emotional scars. Mum would never be forgiven.

I also discovered the world of bear collectors: people of all ages who collect bears for many different reasons, but mostly because the bear had looked at them and said — take me home. There are wealthy collectors who pay enormous sums of money for rare vintage bears, and those who concentrate on modern handmade bears by well-known 'bear artists'. There are many international magazines devoted to teddy bears. There are bear shows, conventions, competitions and auctions held regularly around the world. Teddy bears are fast becoming an art form. Antique bears can be found in important museums in many countries, while modern handmade bears have been exhibited in some very prestigious art galleries.

The teddy bear is so much more than just a soft toy, and this book is more than just a simple make-a-soft-toy book. I would like to show you the world of the teddy bear, where they came from and where they are going. And I would like to show you how to make the best quality bears, in the old-fashioned way and using the traditional materials.

I learned how to make bears the hard way; by myself and by trial-and-error. This book will show you the solutions I have found, and I believe that this is the first time a book on bear-making has covered the subject in such detail. With imagination and perseverence your hobby could easily turn into a career.

CHAPTER 1

THE HISTORY OF THE TEDDY BEAR

Since prehistoric times bears have played an important role in worship, myth, folklore and children's tales. Realistic toy bears became popular in mid-nineteenth century Germany as pull-along toys on wheels, and bears on their hind legs resembling circus bears. It was not, however, until 1902/1903 that the first teddy bear was made. Both the Americans and the Germans claim credit for the first bear, but this is what happened.

In November 1902, the 26th President of the United States, Theodore Roosevelt, went down to settle a border dispute between Mississippi and Louisiana. A keen hunter, he was taken on an unsuccessful bear hunt. The only bear that could be flushed from the woods was so small and pitiful that the President refused to shoot it.

The incident was reported in the Washington Post and the cartoonist Clifford K. Berryman drew a cartoon of Roosevelt and the bear, captioned 'Drawing the Line in Mississippi'. The drawing of the little bear was quite endearing, and the cartoon created quite a stir.

Morris Michtom, a novelty shop owner in Brooklyn, New York, had his wife make some jointed toy bears to sell in their shop. They were a great success and apparently Mr Michtom wrote to the President (who was known personally as Teddy), asking if he could use the President's name and call his toys Teddy's Bears. The President is said to have replied to the effect that he did not think his name would be worth much in the toy bear business, but Michtom was welcome to use it. Michtom's bears were so successful that he went on to form the largest toy business in America, the Ideal Toy Company.

At the same time in Germany the Steiff Company, a small family firm of toymakers, added a stuffed bear to its range. Richard Steiff, a nephew of the founder

3

Margarete Steiff, produced a fully jointed bear for the Leipzig Toy Fair in 1903. There a buyer for the George Borgfeldt Company in New York fell for it and promptly ordered three thousand of them. The Steiff Company never looked back and by 1907 Steiff bear production had reached 975,000 per annum.

The Ideal Company continued until 1982, when it was acquired by CBS Inc., and although the company still produces toys it no longer makes teddy bears. Steiff, on the other hand, continues to make some of the best quality toys and bears in the world today.

Although there may be some confusion as to who actually made the first teddy bear, there is no doubt about their lasting popularity. Teddy bears are here to stay.

DRAWING THE LINE IN MISSISSIPPI

CHAPTER 2

STYLES OF BEARS

Both Ideal and Steiff toy companies had obviously started working on their bear designs in 1902, and by 1903 their bears had emerged into the marketplace. They were, however, very different bears.

Both were fully jointed, made of mohair pile fabric and stuffed with excelsior (wood-wool shavings), but there most of the similarities ended. The American Ideal bear was generally made of a shorter pile mohair than his German counterpart. The head was almost a triangular wedge with rather large, rounded and wide-set ears. The body was a long and narrow sack with a little hump, and the arms and legs were rather straight with fairly small feet. The eyes were small shoe-buttons and the nose was usually horizontally stitched (Fig 1).

The German Steiff bear was designed after careful study of the real animal, and the early Steiffs do seem to display a wonderful subtlety of form. The mohair was often quite shaggy and thick, the shape of the head broad but with a deep, long muzzle or nose. The ears were relatively small and the shoe-button eyes larger than Ideal's. With the exception of the smaller sized bears, Steiff bears generally had vertically stitched noses with the two centre stitches continuing down to join the mouth. The German bear's body was fairly plump with a sway back and a pronounced hump. His arms and legs were long and curved, with tapering wrists and ankles and long feet.

During the early 1900s Steiff exported many bears to England, where British toymakers were quick to latch on to the success of the teddy bear. By 1910 several English toy companies were manufacturing their own bears. They were initially modelled after the American and the German bears but quickly assumed their own identity.

English bears generally had larger heads with shorter muzzles. Their bodies were shorter and plumper, usually without a hump, and their arms and legs shorter, with small rounded feet.

Since its first appearance the teddy bear has undergone many changes in design and materials. Today, manufactured bears are primarily made of acrylic fibre fur and stuffed with polyfill. Their eyes are usually of pop-in plastic and the detailing of embroidered claws is often dispensed with. They are softer, cuddlier and often not even jointed anymore.

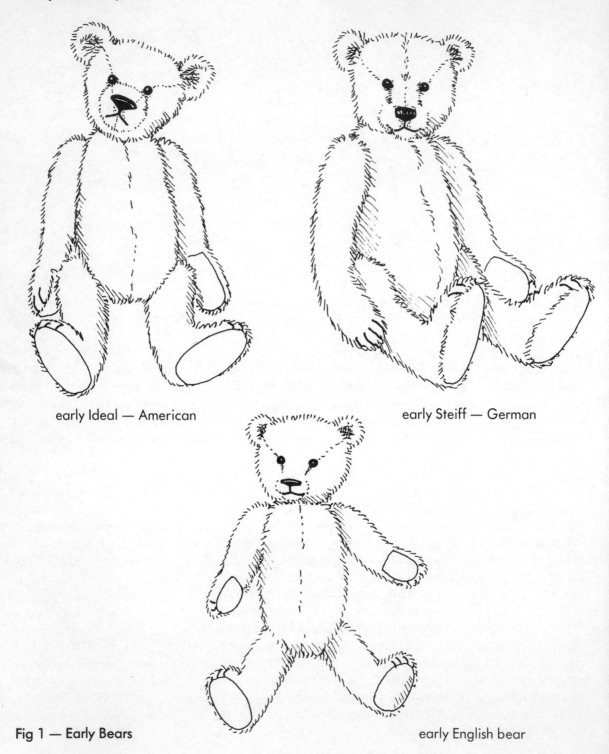

early Ideal — American

early Steiff — German

Fig 1 — Early Bears

early English bear

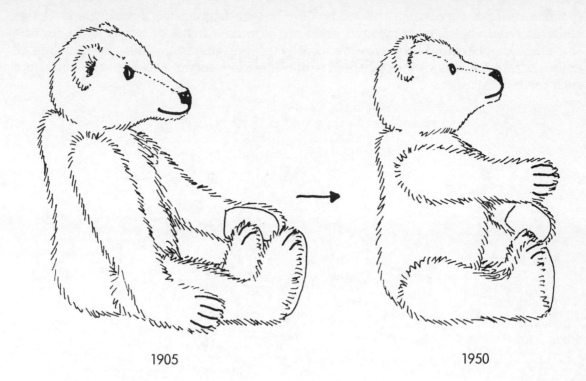

1905   1950

Fig 2 — Changes in proportion over the years

Their proportions have changed dramatically (Fig 2). Over the years their bodies have grown fatter, their heads larger and their limbs shorter and stockier. Their muzzles have also shortened and often they have lost their original real bear look. In many ways the modern teddy bear has forgotten his origins and his ancestors, and lost the intelligence and character he once had.

Steiff has realised this and understands that there is a world of avid bear lovers who appreciate the old-fashioned bears. As prices rise to dizzying heights for the original vintage bears, demand increases for modern affordable replicas. Steiff and some of the other well-known bear companies now release limited edition reproductions of some of their wonderful early bears.

These limited editions are not only highly sought after by the collectors, but they can also be good investments. Apart from manufactured bears, interest has been continually expanding in a relatively new area, that of the individually made bear. 'Real' bears are being made again by creative individuals, not in factories but at home. They are bears with humour glinting in their deep eyes, bears that almost breathe.

1970

CHAPTER 3

ARTIST BEARS AND BEAR ARTISTS

On the West coast of America in the early 1970s the first artist bears were created. The artists often had dollmaking backgrounds and the first bears appeared at doll conventions. They were a great success and bear-making went from strength to strength. Now there are teddy bear clubs, shops, shows, conventions, magazines and books to be found around the world.

In the USA alone there are now hundreds of individuals making full-time careers out of creating their own special kind of bear. Not every handmade bear can be considered to be an artist bear, though, and not every bear-maker is a bear artist.

In order for a bear to be an artist bear, it must be completely created by the artist. The maker is not just a hobbyist or craftsperson, but someone who has an artistic vision and viewpoint, and can express that creatively with expertise. An artist's personal creative forces should produce something that is quite unique.

Whether their special bears are sewn by machine or by hand, bear artists make them in small numbers, often in limited editions. The best artists have recognisable personal styles that are innovative and constantly evolving.

Modern bear-making can fall into one of several categories.

- Hand-stitchers who do everything themselves, from the design to the finished bear. Production is slow and very limited due to the time involved. Bears are often one-of-a-kind, and there is commonly a long waiting list for these bears.

- Bear-makers who design and make the bear alone, but use a sewing machine. This speeds up production, but even so, the output rarely exceeds one or two bears a day. Bears are still often very limited editions, with demand usually exceeding supply.

- Bear-makers who have assistance with sewing or with various stages of construction, although they design the bear and personally do the final details such as the face. With such a cottage industry, production is greatly increased, but with other people involved, quality may suffer.

- Designers who may design the bear but have it made by a company, either their own or someone else's. The designers might have their names on the tags, but they are not involved in the making of the bear, and this cannot be considered to be an artist bear.

CHAPTER 4

MATERIALS

Teddy bears can be made out of many things, but in this book we will mainly be concerned with using the traditional materials. They are the best quality and the most long-lasting, but unfortunately are also often the most expensive.

Practise with cheaper materials at first, and when you are ready, use the best. It will be well worth the extra expense, and with careful cutting you can make even the most expensive fabric go a long way. The best fabric of all is, of course — mohair.

MOHAIR

This is the long, strong hair of the angora goat and has been used in all types of textiles since biblical days. The main countries of mohair production today are the USA, South Africa and Turkey, but Australia and New Zealand are now also producing top quality mohair.

Mohair is used for many things, from knitting wool to wigs and velour upholstery fabric. In the old days a woven pile mohair fabric was often used for coats. Now this style of mohair is made almost exclusively for teddy bears.

Mohair pile fabric comes in many different colours, lengths and densities. It may even be tipped with another colour or wavy (distressed). It also tends to be wider than most materials (143 cm, 57″) so if another fabric is used, allow extra for your patterns. Once you have found your supplier, obtain sample swatches of all the available types and decide how you want your bear to look.

The length of the fur can make a dramatic difference to the overall appearance of the bear. If it is too short, he may look bristly and thin; if it is too long, he will look very fat and his features may seem too small.

A good basic ratio to follow is this:

Bear size	Fur length
3–6″ (7.5–15 cm)	¼″ (0.5 cm)
6–8″ (15–20 cm)	⅜″ (1 cm)
9–10″ (22.5–25 cm)	½″ (1.5 cm)
11–13″ (28–33 cm)	¾″ (2 cm)
14″+ (35.5 cm +)	1″+ (2.5 cm)

(PLEASE NOTE THAT METRIC MEASUREMENTS THROUGHOUT HAVE BEEN ROUNDED TO THE NEAREST 0.5 CM.)

This, of course, just gives you a rough idea to start with. The whole idea of making your own bear is to do it your way, so experiment.

The nap of the fur is the direction your hand goes when you smooth it down. When you ruffle it up you are pushing against the nap. Always find the nap on your piece of fabric and mark it with an arrow on the reverse side. This will make it easier to lay out your pattern, and will result in a finished bear with a realistic flowing look to his fur, much like a real animal.

EYES

In the early years, teddy bears' eyes were shoe- or boot-buttons, but by around 1910 specially made glass eyes on loops or wires were introduced. Today most commercially made bears have 'safety-lock' plastic eyes. If you are making a collectible bear rather than a child's bear, try using glass eyes or, if you can find them, old shoe-buttons.

Glass eyes may have to be matched up for pupil size and overall shape as they are handmade and all slightly different. They come in all sizes and colours.

Shoe-button or boot-button eyes are from antique boots and are becoming increasingly scarce. They are usually black leather-covered steel buttons on a loop back. If you can find them, they are wonderful to use and give the bear a softer, old-fashioned look.

A rough guideline of eye size to bear size is:

Bear size	Eye size
3–6" (7.5–15 cm)	3–5 mm
6–8" (15–20 cm)	5–7 mm
9–10" (22.5–25 cm)	8–9 mm
11–12" (28–30 cm)	10–11 mm
13–15" (33–35 cm)	12–14 mm

Of course, a lot depends on your overall proportions, size of head, length of fur, expression, etc. Bear in mind (excuse the pun) that in general, smaller eyes impart more character and look better than eyes which are too large.

PAW PADS

Traditionally teddy bears' paws were made of a good thick felt, although suede and leather feel nice and last well too. Today paws can be made from a wide range of fabrics, but we will concentrate on using felt to begin with.

JOINTS

There are several ways to make joints for a teddy bear, but they all use the same basic units of discs and washers (Fig 3).

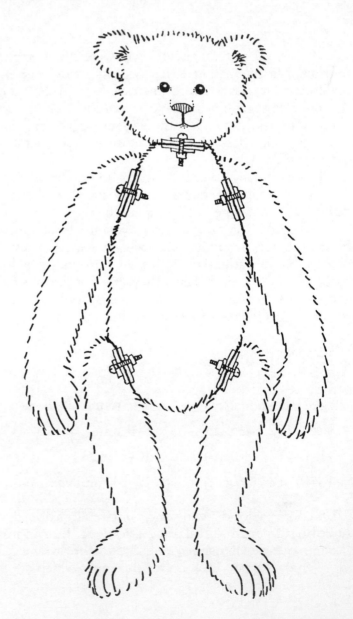

Fig 3 — Joint placement

DISCS

These may be made from plastic, cardboard, hardboard (a composite material) or plywood. The size of the discs used is important, for it affects the overall look of the bear and the movement of his joints. If the discs are too small for the bear, his limbs will be wobbly and his shoulders and hips will be large and bulbous. If, on the other hand, they are too large, they may not fit into his limbs at all.

If you are designing your own pattern, you can easily work out which size discs you will need. Allow a ¼″ (0.5 cm) margin around the inner seam edge of the shoulder or hip section of your pattern and draw a circle of the corresponding size. This circle will be your disc size, and the centre of it will be where you mark the joint placing on the pattern (Fig 4).

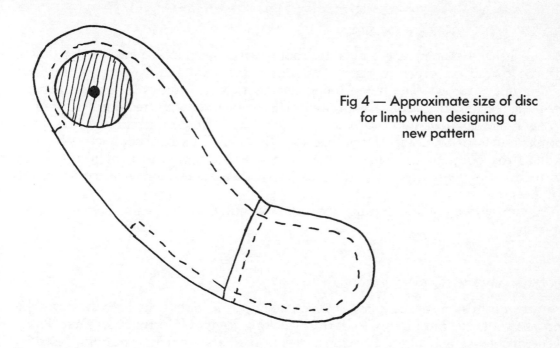

Fig 4 — Approximate size of disc for limb when designing a new pattern

WASHERS

For each bear, you will need ten discs and ten smaller washers. These are usually of non-rusting metal and enable each joint to move smoothly. For bears under 8″ (20 cm), washers alone are usually all that is needed.

The discs and washers are held by one of several jointing options (Fig 5).

crown joint with split pin

split pin joint

locknut and bolt joint

Fig 5

COTTER PINS OR SPLIT PINS

These pins are fitted through the discs and washers and the ends are bent open or rolled down to hold the joint in place. Cotter pins are good for jointing small bears, but with large heavy bears the joints may loosen a little over time.

POP RIVET

A special tool is used to rivet a metal pin through the discs. This provides a firm, long-lasting joint, although it takes some practice. If a mistake is made it can be very difficult to dismantle the joint in order to re-do it.

SELF-LOCKING NUTS OR NYLOC NUTS

These are usually stainless steel nuts and bolts, with the nuts having a nylon lining inside the thread. In order to tighten or loosen the joint the bolt has to be held while the nut is turned. The nylon lining ensures that the nuts will never loosen by themselves, resulting in a strong, lasting joint that can be finely adjusted during assembly.

We will be using locknuts and bolts in this book, but note that for the neck joint a normal nut is being used. This is because the head is already complete when we joint it to the body, so we cannot hold the bolt end in order to tighten a locknut. A normal nut is tightened to the desired degree then superglued in place to ensure that it does not slip.

There are several other jointing options in making teddy bears that are worth mentioning.

POP JOINTS OR PLASTIC DOLL JOINTS

These are mushroom-shaped plastic pieces with plastic discs which 'pop' onto the ridged shaft of the mushroom to form a locking joint. Unfortunately these joints are generally loose and not very strong, although this system is commonly used in manufactured soft toys today. They do have the advantage of being fully washable.

LOC-LINE

This is a new invention of a modular system of interlocking plastic pieces which become an internal skeleton instead of separate joints. Loc-line was developed for bear artists and allows one to create new bears with bendable limbs that can be posed. Standard patterns may need adjustment in order to use this system.

SWIVEL NECK JOINTS

Another new system, this was developed by a Californian bear artist to enable a bear's head to be tilted up, down or to either side. Again, standard patterns may need adjustment and the mechanisms are for bears over 14″ (35.5 cm).

STUFFING

Your bear's final appearance will depend largely on what you use to stuff him.

EXCELSIOR

The earliest bears were very firmly stuffed with excelsior or wood-wool shavings. This is difficult to work with, is not washable and today is not often used. If you decide to use excelsior, cut it into manageable pieces first, then roll it into a cigar shape betwen your hands before packing it in firmly with your stuffing tool.

KAPOK

This is another natural and non-washable stuffing material. It was commonly used in English bear manufacture before the introduction of synthetics. It can be difficult to work with as it tends to clump, and can be heavy in large bears.

RAW SHEEP'S WOOL

This can make a good lightweight filling material and is washable. As it is so springy it is good for softly stuffed bears, but may not pack down well if you are aiming for a firmly stuffed one. The fleece should be washed before being used to remove oil and dirt.

Remember to allow for the size of the growler, etc when sewing up the body so that a large enough opening for insertion is left during stuffing. The stem and key for a music box usually protrudes from the back and the back seam is closed around it.

POLYESTER AND DACRON FIBREFILL

These are the most commonly used stuffing materials today. They are found readily in handicraft shops and are easy to use. Different brands have different qualities, so find one that you like to work with. Some are very slippery and springy and will not pack down easily; these are best suited to softly stuffed bears.

PLASTIC PELLETS

These are solid little beads and are often used in artist bear production. They are not classified as childproof, so do not use them if making children's bears. In a collector's bear, however, when used in conjunction with polyfill, pellets give a lovely weight and a malleable feel. (Even in a pellet bear, the head is always firmly stuffed with polyfill to keep its shape.)

GROWLERS, SQUEAKERS AND MUSIC BOXES

These are all wonderful mechanisms that can add an extra dimension to your bear by providing him with a voice. The best ones still come from Germany and Switzerland, although some are available from Japan and China also.

If you wish to use a growler, squeaker or music box in your bear, he must have a large enough body to accommodate it. The body must also be well stuffed to avoid the mechanism shifting or its edges being felt.

Remember to allow for the size of the growler, etc. when sewing up the body so that a large enough opening for insertion is left during stuffing. The stem and key for a music box usually protrudes from the back and the back seam is closed around it.

If using a squeaker, remember that it will have to be placed close to the bear's front, as its tummy is pressed to activate it.

If using a growler, cover the air holes at the top with a piece of very fine cloth first. This will stop any stuffing from entering and clogging the mechanism. When it is inserted into the middle of the body, make sure that the airholes are facing the neck joint or the growler will be upside down. The bear should growl when lifted upright.

PLATE 1

PLATE 2

PLATE 3

PLATE 4

PLATE 5

CHAPTER 5

TOOLS

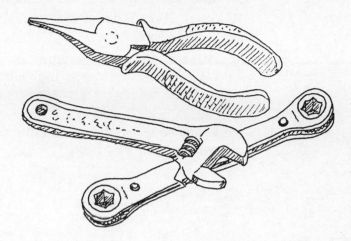

There are very few specialised tools needed to make teddy bears. Most items can be found at home or purchased from a craft or hardware shop. Here is a list of the most useful items:

Needles: A variety of sizes and lengths, from darners to large dollmaking needles for sewing in eyes; these are usually from 3″ (7.5 cm) to 8″ (20 cm) long. Leather needles will also be needed if you are hand-sewing leather or suede for paw pads.

Pins: Glass-headed berry pins are long, thin and the easiest to work with.

Thimble: Very useful for working with leather.

Scissors: A good pair of sharp, pointed scissors is essential, and they should be fairly small and easy to handle.

Apron: This is a good idea, otherwise all your clothes will end up covered in hair, and strangers will ask you what type of animals you keep.

Marking pens: Waterproof laundry markers are ideal for drawing the patterns onto the fabric. Water-soluble ones tend to run if glue is being used on the seam openings.

Pliers: A small pair of fine-nosed pliers is often very handy in assisting with stubborn needles and tricky positions.

Glue: Various types of glue are needed in bear production: superglue for the neck joint, some watered down PVA in a squeeze bottle for the seam edgings, and some tacky vinyl or leather glue for attaching the nose templates.

Awl: A sharp knitting needle will also do, for making eye holes and joint holes without tearing the fabric.

Wooden chopsticks: Excellent stuffing tools, as are wooden spoon handles.

Spanners: Ratchet spanners or dumbbell-shaped bicycle spanners are easiest for tightening nut and bolt joints. Small adjustable wrenches are also useful.

Brush: A small, wire dog brush is very good for grooming your old bears and for getting the fur out of seams in your new bears.

CHAPTER 6

INGREDIENTS

PATTERN ONE

A basic 8″ (20 cm) fully jointed bear with a two-piece body and one-piece arms and legs.

Mohair Fabric: 15 cm/⅛ yd of 1 cm/⅜″ pile length

Eyes: One pair of 7 or 8 mm/⁵⁄₁₆″ glass on wire loop shanks

Paws: 7.5 cm/3″ square of felt

Washers: Ten 2 cm/¾″ zinc with a 5 mm/³⁄₁₆″ hole

Hexagonal Bolts: Five 5 mm/³⁄₁₆″, 2 cm/¾″ long

Nyloc Hexagonal Nuts: Four 5 mm/³⁄₁₆″ (self-locking)

Hexagonal Nut: One 5 mm/³⁄₁₆″

Thread: DMC No. 8 in a matching colour is a good strong thread for hand-sewing. DMC No. 5 in a suitable brown or black is good for the nose

Stuffing: A small bag of polyfill/dacron stuffing

PATTERN TWO

A 12" (30 cm) old-fashioned bear, with long arms and legs, and a four-piece body.

Mohair Fabric: 25 cm/¼ yd of 2 cm/¾" pile

Eyes: One pair of 9 or 10 mm/⅜" glass of boot-button eyes

Paws: 15 cm/6" square of felt or leather

Discs: Ten 38 mm/1½" hardboard discs

Washers: Ten 2 cm/¾" zinc washers, 7 mm/¼" holes

Hexagonal Bolts: Five 7 mm/¼" by 25 mm/1" long

Nyloc Hexagonal Nuts: Four 7 mm/¼"

Hexagonal Nut: One 7 mm/¼"

Thread: DMC No. 8 for sewing. DMC No. 5 for the nose

Stuffing: A pillow-sized bag of polyfill stuffing

PATTERN THREE

A 16" (40 cm) character bear, with bent arms and legs.

Mohair Fabric: 50 cm/½ yd or 25 mm/1" pile

Eyes: One pair of 12 mm/½" glass eyes

Paws: 15 cm/6" square of felt

Discs: Ten 45 mm/1¾" hardboard discs

Washers: Ten 2 cm/¾" zinc washers, with 7 mm/¼" hole

Hexagonal Bolts: Five 7 mm/¼"

Nyloc Hexagonal Nuts: Four 7 mm/¼"

Hexagonal Nut: One 7 mm/¼"

Threads: DMC No. 8 for sewing and DMC No. 5 or 3 for the nose and claws

Stuffing: A large bag of polyfill stuffing

CHAPTER 7

PATTERNS

Y ou have your materials and you have chosen your pattern. Each of the three patterns in this book increases in complexity, so if this is your first attempt at bear-making, I suggest you try Pattern One first.

Each pattern can be enlarged or decreased in size using the grid pattern indicated (Fig 6), so from these three patterns a whole range of bears can be created. As your confidence in bear-making increases, use your imagination to change these patterns. Modify areas to achieve new looks; for example, a longer muzzle, bigger feet, smaller eyes, larger ears. Eventually you will be able to design confidently your own patterns to produce the bears of your dreams.

When designing your own patterns there are some basic proportions that should be borne in mind. These are not hard and fast rules, but will help you to produce a balanced-looking bear.

BASIC PROPORTIONS

The length of the body should be around twice the height of the head. A larger head will give the effect of a younger bear, a smaller head the look of an older bear.

The limbs should be at least as long as the body. Early bears had limbs even longer than the body. The arms look best if they are slightly longer than the legs.

If the body is fairly chubby or thick around the middle then the shoulders and thighs should be slightly heavier to balance the overall look.

The paw and foot pad width should be fairly equal, no matter what shape or size, in order to balance the limbs.

If a bear is to be fully clothed, his proportions will need to be altered. Most bears are rather tubby, and if you wish to design a dressed bear, you might think of slimming down the bodyline and lengthening the legs.

Looking at our patterns, some basic concepts emerge. The three-piece head pattern is the most common, although some bears may have six or more sections making up their heads. This is especially true when making a head with an inset muzzle of a contrasting fabric.

The body pattern may be of two, three or four pieces. Our first pattern has a two-piece body, but much more subtlety of shape can be achieved using four pieces to make up the body. The stuffing opening is usually left at the back, and there is also a neck opening. In some cases the stuffing is done through the neck, but then the jointing of the head may be a problem.

The arms and legs are often designed in one piece, leaving less seams to show. If however, you are designing a bear with elbows and knees, you will need to use two-piece patterns as we do with our Pattern Three. The stuffing openings for the limbs are usually nearest the jointing area, for ease of access. Some bears' limbs are stuffed from the top of the shoulder and thigh, but it is easier to close the seam when it is straight rather than on a curve such as a shoulder.

ENLARGING YOUR PATTERNS

Draw a diagonal line through the pattern outline and extend the line past the corner (Fig 7). Extend from the vertical left margin of the pattern to the size required. (For example, you can double or triple it.) Draw a horizontal line at the base to intersect the diagonal line, giving two sides of the enlarged shape. Draw up the remaining sides, divide the area into the same number of grid sections and copy the outline from each corresponding section. This will give you the enlarged pattern.

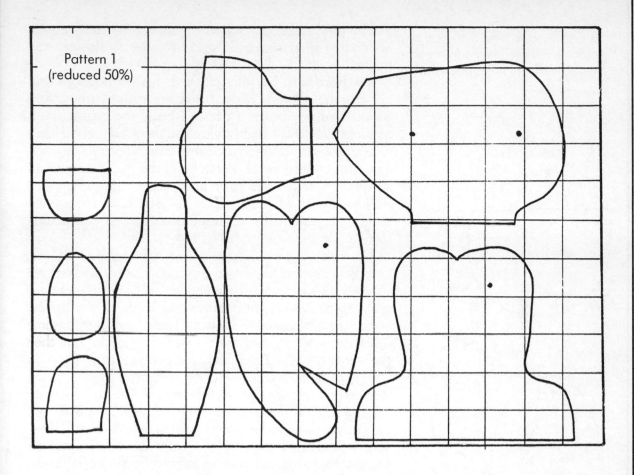

Pattern 1
(reduced 50%)

**Fig 6 — Reducing and enlarging a pattern
by putting it on a grid**

Fig 7 — Enlarging a pattern on a grid

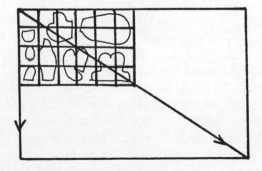

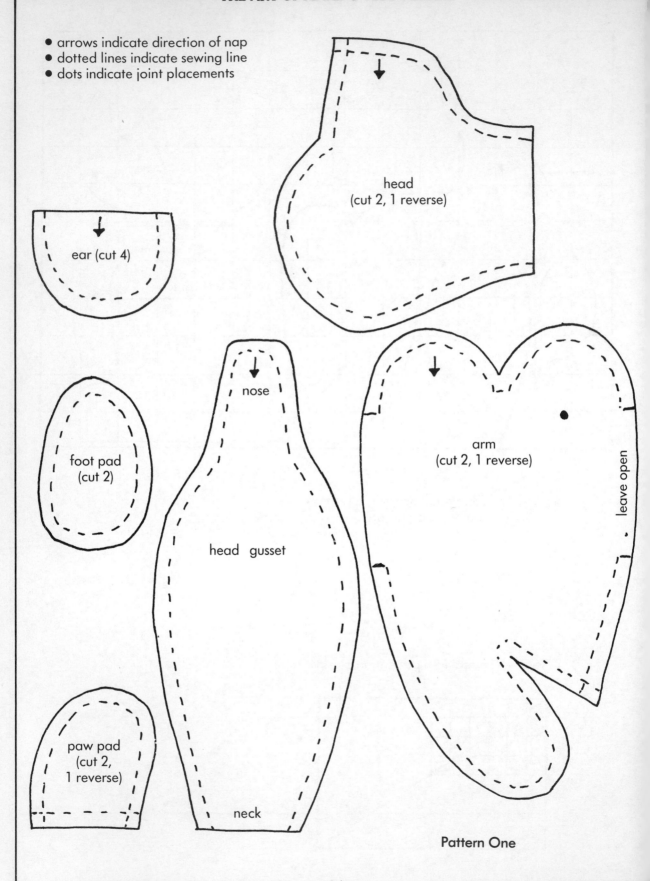

- arrows indicate direction of nap
- dotted lines indicate sewing line
- dots indicate joint placements

ear (cut 4)

head
(cut 2, 1 reverse)

foot pad
(cut 2)

nose

arm
(cut 2, 1 reverse)

leave open

head gusset

paw pad
(cut 2,
1 reverse)

neck

Pattern One

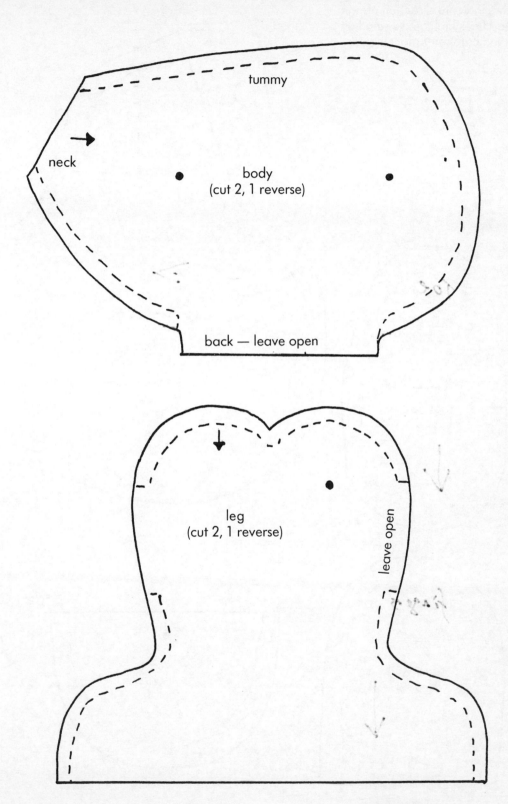

tummy

neck

body
(cut 2, 1 reverse)

back — leave open

leg
(cut 2, 1 reverse)

leave open

Pattern One

- arrows indicate direction of nap
- dotted lines indicate sewing line
- dots indicate joint placements

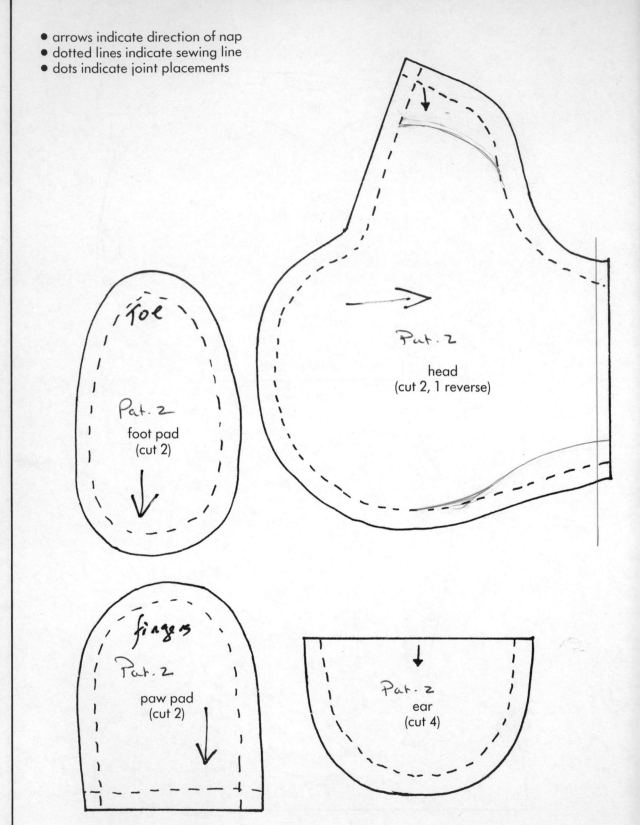

Toe

Pat. 2
foot pad
(cut 2)

Pat. 2
head
(cut 2, 1 reverse)

fingers

Pat. 2
paw pad
(cut 2)

Pat. 2
ear
(cut 4)

Pattern Two

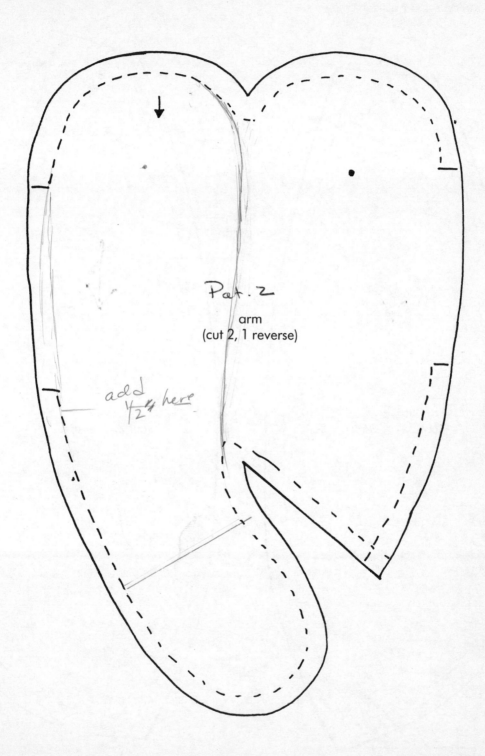

Pat. 2
arm
(cut 2, 1 reverse)

add
1/2" here

Pattern Two

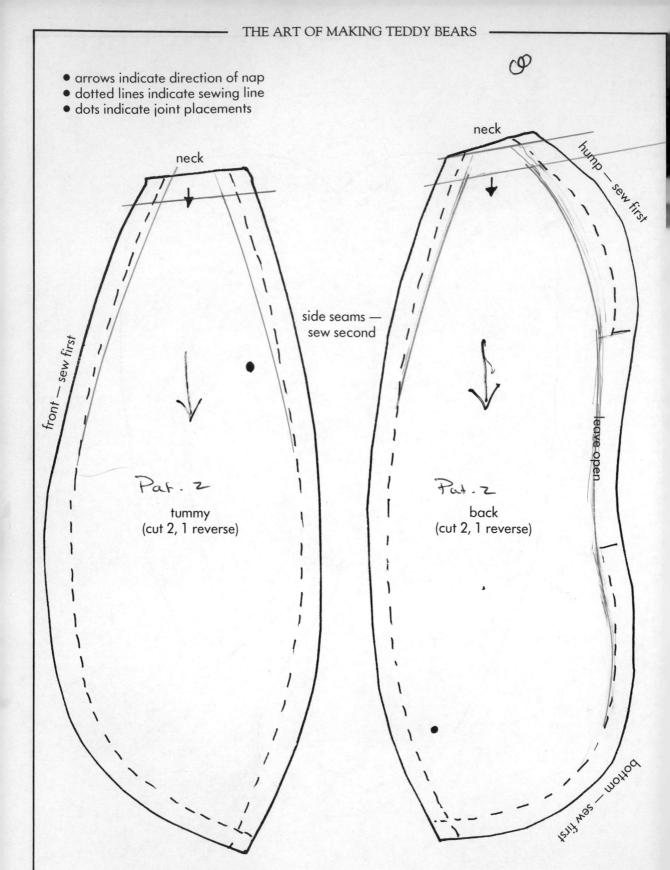

- arrows indicate direction of nap
- dotted lines indicate sewing line
- dots indicate joint placements

neck

neck

hump — sew first

side seams —
sew second

front — sew first

leave open

Pat. 2

tummy
(cut 2, 1 reverse)

Pat. 2

back
(cut 2, 1 reverse)

bottom — sew first

Pattern Two

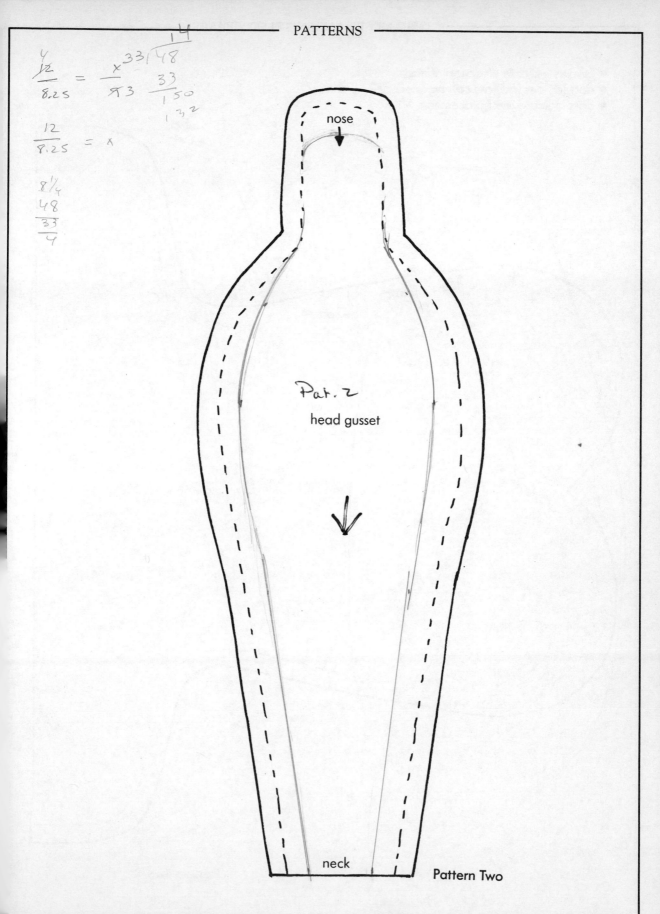

$$\frac{4}{12}$$
$$\frac{12}{8.25} = \frac{x}{83} \quad 33\overline{)48} \quad \frac{14}{33}$$
$$\frac{33}{150}$$
$$132$$

$$\frac{12}{8.25} = x$$

$$8\frac{1}{4}$$
$$48$$
$$33$$
$$\overline{4}$$

nose

Pat. 2

head gusset

neck

Pattern Two

- arrows indicate direction of nap
- dotted lines indicate sewing line
- dots indicate joint placements

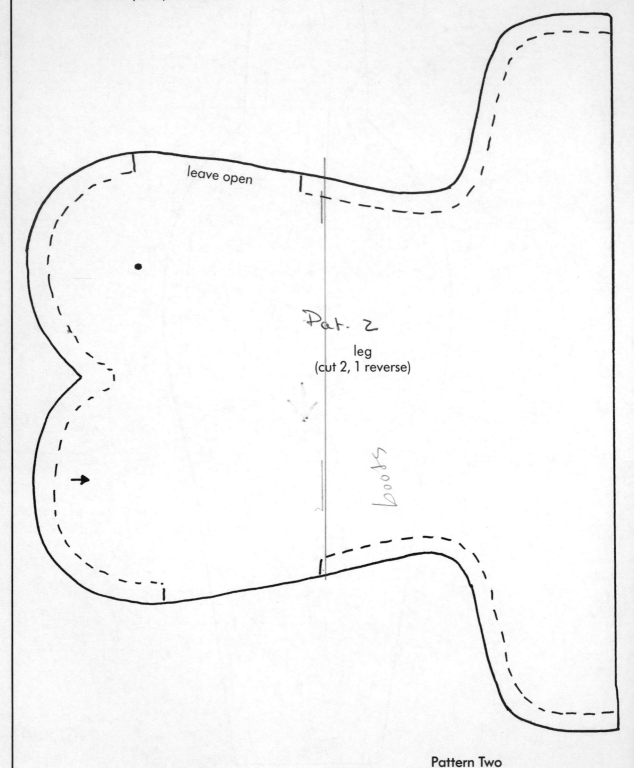

leave open

Pat. 2

leg
(cut 2, 1 reverse)

boots

Pattern Two

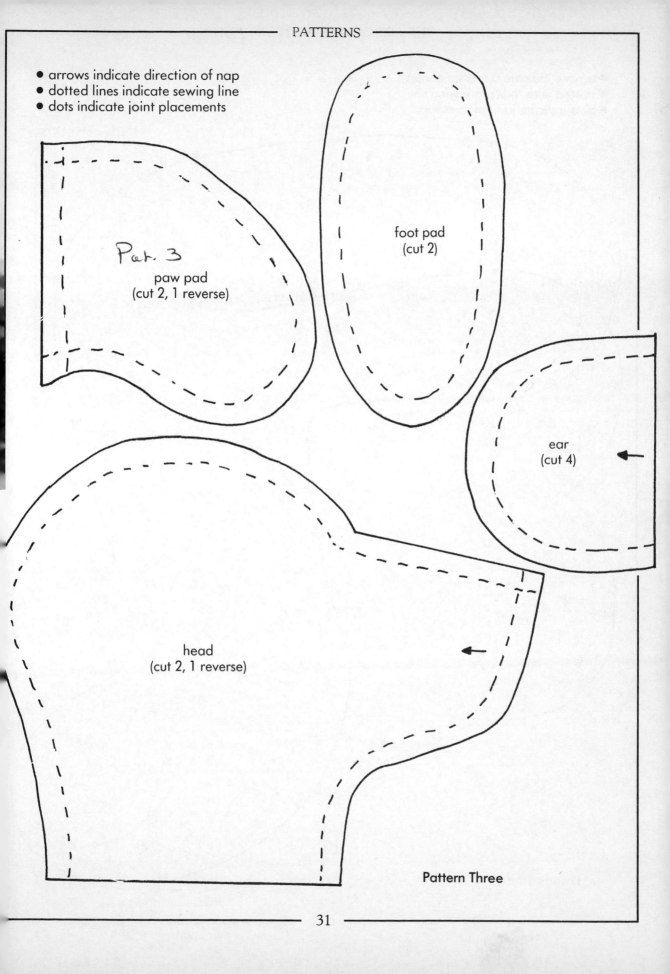

- arrows indicate direction of nap
- dotted lines indicate sewing line
- dots indicate joint placements

Pat. 3

paw pad
(cut 2, 1 reverse)

foot pad
(cut 2)

ear
(cut 4)

head
(cut 2, 1 reverse)

Pattern Three

- arrows indicate direction of nap
- dotted lines indicate sewing line
- dots indicate joint placements

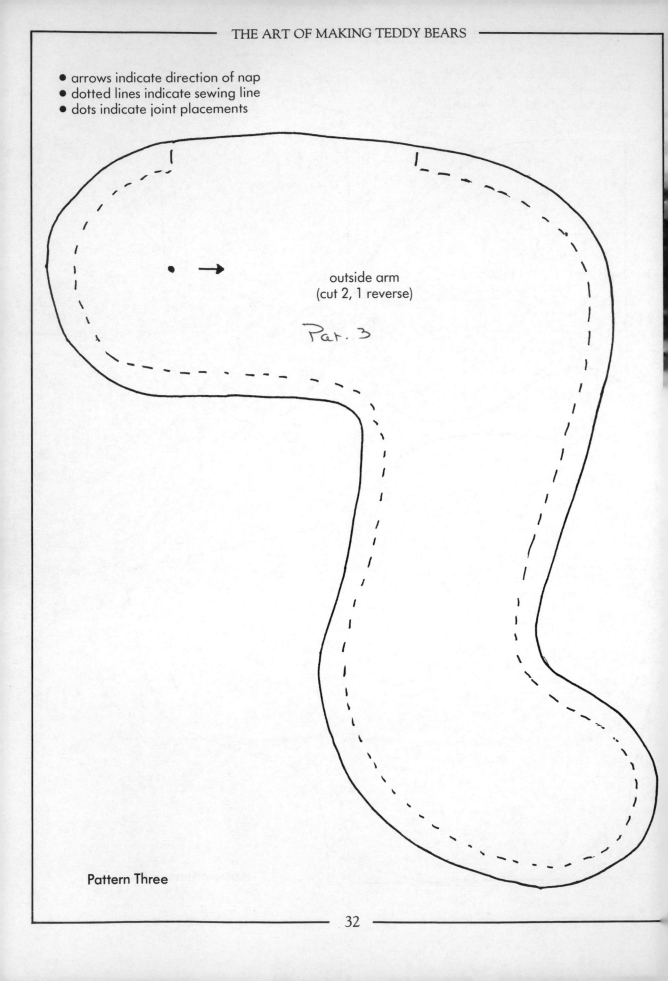

outside arm
(cut 2, 1 reverse)

Pat. 3

Pattern Three

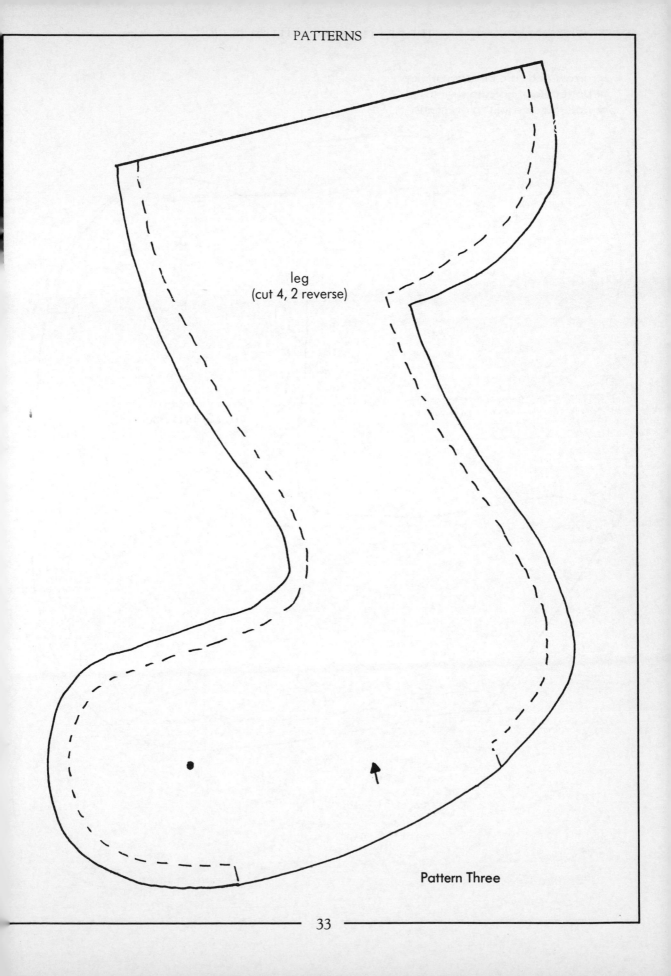

leg
(cut 4, 2 reverse)

Pattern Three

- arrows indicate direction of nap
- dotted lines indicate sewing line
- dots indicate joint placements

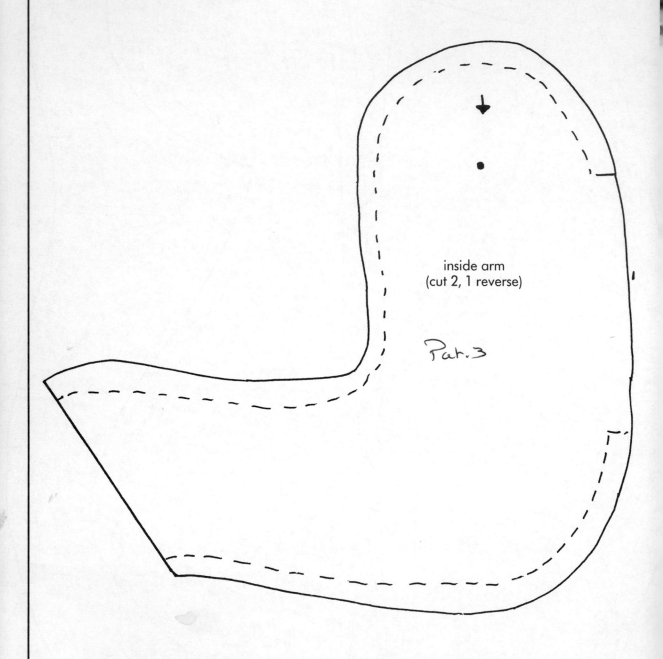

inside arm
(cut 2, 1 reverse)

Pat. 3

Pattern Three

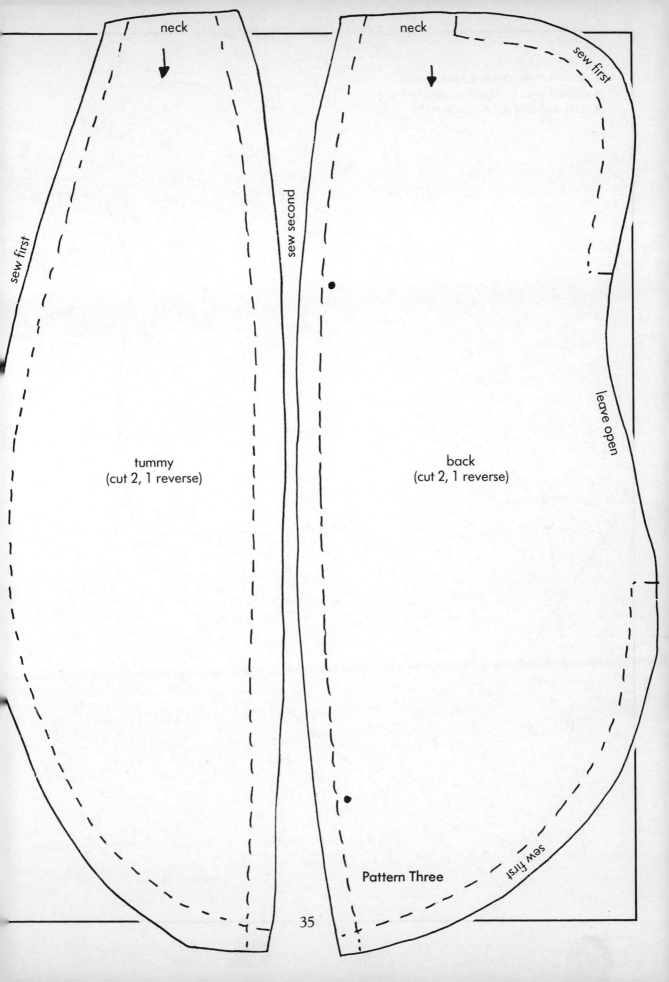

neck

sew first

sew second

tummy
(cut 2, 1 reverse)

neck

sew first

leave open

back
(cut 2, 1 reverse)

Pattern Three

sew first

35

- arrows indicate direction of nap
- dotted lines indicate sewing line
- dots indicate joint placements

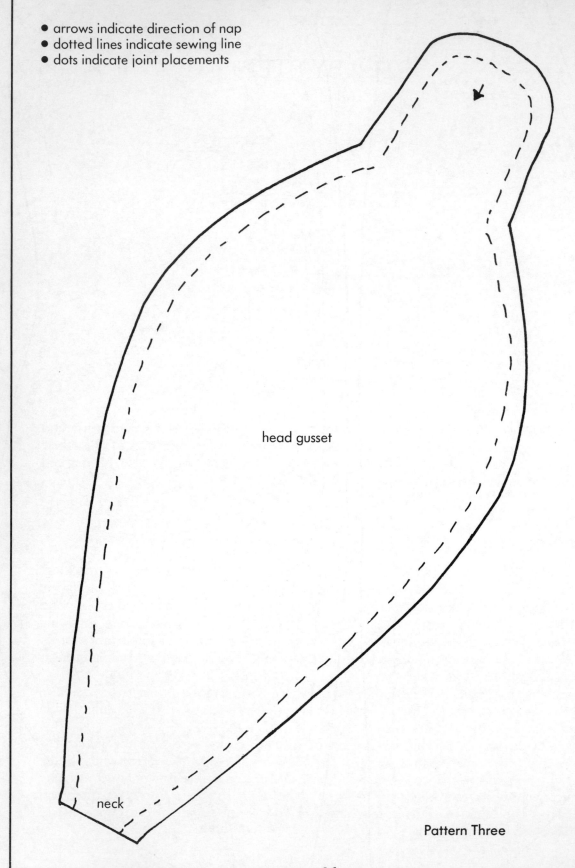

head gusset

neck

Pattern Three

CHAPTER 8

STEP BY STEP

If you plan on using your pattern more than once, transfer it to cardboard and label each piece. Remember that arrows indicate the nap or direction of the fabric pile, and dotted lines indicate sewing. Openings for stuffing should also be marked until you are confident about where they should be.

LAYING OUT THE PATTERN

The pattern pieces are always laid out on the back of the fabric for ease of marking. Find the nap, mark its direction with a little arrow on the reverse side of the fabric and take time in laying out your pattern shapes. The arrows on them should correspond with the arrow on the fabric. You will find that it is like a jigsaw puzzle in trying to fit your pattern in economically. As mohair is not cheap it is important not to waste any of your fabric. It is a good idea to save any offcuts that may be big enough to use again.

Check that you have reversed the pieces where this is required, so that you have a proper pair before you cut them out. Mark around the edges closely with an indelible felt pen, remembering to mark the joint holes as you go.

If you are using an acrylic fur instead of mohair, make sure that the fabric has a woven backing rather than a knitted one. This means that the fabric will not be so stretchy and will not distort when the bear is stuffed. If you can only get stretchy fabric to begin with, you might try using spray adhesive to glue a thin layer of cotton material on the back of the fur fabric before laying out your pattern. This should stop the fabric from distorting.

CUTTING OUT

Use a small pair of sharp, pointed scissors. On a flat surface, take small careful snips, cutting only the fabric backing and not the fur pile. If you rush through the cutting or take big snips, you may chop the fur and it will show up on the finished seams.

The seams should be completely hidden if the fabric has been well cut and the fur pulled out of the seams after turning — a sign of a well-made bear.

PINNING

The pieces are all sewn inside out. They are first pinned together with the fur tucked in, then oversewn with a simple overcast stitch to act as a tacking and keep the pieces in position. The pins may be removed as you go. Make sure that you use plenty of pins as the pieces will move as you sew and could otherwise end up misaligned.

Note: Pin the pieces together with the heads of the pins to the outside and the points pointing in to the middle of the piece. This will keep the piece flat and easy to work with (Fig 8).

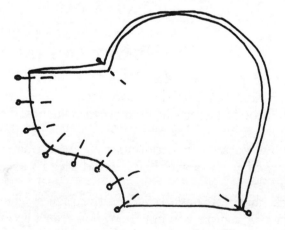

Fig 8 — Pinning in preparation for
the first seam of the head, from
the tip of the nose down to the neck

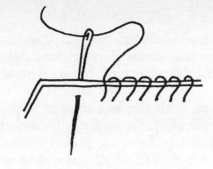

overcasting or oversewing,
for tacking pieces together

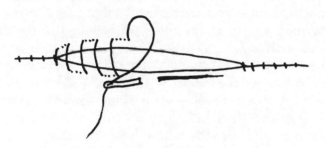

backstitch or reverse stitch,
for sewing seams

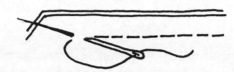

ladder stitch, for closing
seams after stuffing

Fig 9 — Stitches

STITCHING

The stitches used in sewing your bear are very simple. They are overcasting, which you have already done to tack your pieces together, backstitch or reverse stitch to form the seam, and ladder stitch to close the openings after stuffing (Fig 9).

Unlike tacking, the overcasting is left to give extra seam strength. Using a small reverse stitch or backstitch, sew the pieces, allowing a 6 mm/¼" seam from the edge. If you stitch any closer to the edge, it may rip when you are stuffing.

To close final openings after stuffing, an invisible stitch called ladder stitch is used. Pushing a 6 mm/¼" edge inside, stitch across the opening and come up on that side again. Cross over and repeat, drawing your stitches tight so that your seam pulls together and no thread shows.

SEWING

In this book we are showing you how to make a hand-stitched bear, but there is no reason why your bear could not be machine sewn. If you are using thick fur, however, it is still best to do the overcasting first by hand before sewing the seam on the machine.

The main thing to remember when sewing with fur is that it is much easier to sew in the direction of the nap than against it. The fur is easier to tuck in and pin flat, and you won't be fighting against its grain.

Starting with the head is a good idea as it is a difficult shape and it is important to sew it accurately.

THE HEAD

Pin the two head pieces together and sew firstly from the tip of the nose down to the front neck edge. Then pin in the head gusset by pinning each eye corner and the middle of the nose tip to centre it. Use more pins around the nose and stitch the U-shape of the muzzle from one eye spot to the other. By sewing just the nose at first enables you to make sure that it is straight and even.

Next, pin in the back of the head, starting at the neck edge on each side and working toward the nose. Each side can then be stitched. You may find that if you pin in and sew the whole head gusset at once the nose may end up being off-centre. It is very important to set in the muzzle accurately or the whole face of the finished bear will be distorted.

The head can then be turned right side out by pushing the nose through the neck opening. Pick the fur out of the seams with a needle and put the head aside.

THE BODY

Pattern One has a two-piece body that is easily pinned. Sew from the front neck edge down and around to the bottom of the back opening, and from the back neck edge down to the top of the back opening. Using your diluted PVA glue in a squeeze bottle, run a 6mm/¼" strip of glue along the edges of the back opening to stiffen them. Let dry and then turn the body right side out through the back opening.

With Patterns Two and Three the body has four pieces. Start with the two tummy pieces; pin flat and sew from the front of the neck down to the bottom edge. Do the same with the two back pieces, allowing an adequate gap (about three fingers wide) for the back

PLATE 6

PLATE 7

PLATE 8

PLATE 9

PLATE 10

PLATE 11

PLATE 12

PLATE 13

opening. Sew from the neck over the hump to the top of the opening, and from below the opening to the bottom edge.

Pin the completed front and back halves together, making sure that the bottom meeting place of all four seams is centred. Sew each side down from the top, carefully tucking in all the fur at the bottom. Again, run glue along the open seam edges, let dry and turn the body right side out. Pick out the fur from the seams with a needle or brush.

THE EARS

For each of the ears, pin two halves together and oversew. Because of the curve and the fur you may find that ears can be tricky to do neatly. Before backstitching the seam, turn the ear out and pick out the fur that may be caught up. When you turn it back, you will find it easier to sew. When you have finished the seam, knot the thread but leave it hanging. When you turn the ear out, the thread will be used to sew the open edges under and to attach it to the head.

ARMS

Whether using a one- or two-piece arm pattern, the first thing to stitch is the wrist of the paw pad to the inner arm. Pin the straight edges together and sew across. If using felt, it does not matter which side faces in, but remember which side you want to show if using leather or suede.

Pin the sides of the arm together if using two pieces, or fold it in and pin if using one piece. Leaving the stuffing opening at the back of the arm as indicated on the pattern, sew all around the arm and paw in the direction of the fur, that is, from the top down.

Run glue along the opening, let dry and turn out, starting with the tip of the paw and gently using your chopstick or stuffing tool. Limbs can be quite awkward to turn, especially in small bears, so take your time and be careful not to poke your stick through the paw.

LEGS

Unlike the arms, the paw pad for the legs is fitted in after the leg is sewn. Fold the leg together if using a one piece pattern or place the pieces together if using a two piece pattern and pin all around. Leaving the stuffing opening and the bottom of the foot open, sew from the top of the leg down.

Place in the foot pad, centering it with pins first at the tip of the toe and the middle of the heel, then pins at the sides. Sew it in, starting from the top. Run glue along the edges of the leg seam opening, let dry and turn out. Your bear is now ready for stuffing and assembling.

STUFFING

We will start with the most important and difficult part of the bear, his head. With all stuffing, remember to begin with the 'corners', that is, the nose, the toes, the paws and the shoulders. If you don't stuff these parts well at the start you will not be able to reach them again once you fill the rest of that body part. A badly stuffed bear will look and feel amateurish and it can detract from his value as well as his appeal.

Stuffing always takes more time and polyfill than you think it will, especially if you want a firm-feeling bear. Even if you want a softer bear his head should always be hard packed to ensure that his features do not distort when he is played with.

THE HEAD

Starting with the nose, pack small pieces of stuffing in very firmly with your stuffing tool. Use your hand around the nose as you stuff it to make sure that you don't poke too hard, and constantly feel for lumps or gaps. Work slowly back to fill the rest of the head.

When the head is stuffed to your satisfaction, pack the stuffing into the neck to form a flat base, allowing the fabric to extend a little further than the stuffing. The neck joint can now be sewn in place, using the right sized hardware for the bear you are making.

On a screw, place a metal washer followed by a hardboard disc (if making Pattern Two or Three). Place this in the centre of the opening with the screw extending from the hole. Using a double sewing thread put a running stitch around the neck 6 mm/¼" from the edge and gather it in firmly. Sew the edges together around the screw with a darning stitch and knot off.

The eyes: The head is now ready for the eyes. Decide where you want the eyes, using pins to mark the position. Use an awl or a pointed knitting needle to poke a hole large enough to take the shank (on the back of the eye). Thread an eye onto a strong cord (often DMC Nos. 3 or 5, which you will be using for the nose, will be fine) and thread both ends onto a long doll needle. The needle must be long enough to reach diagonally through the head.

Going in through the eye hole you have made, bring the needle out at the back of the neck as close to the edge of the disc as possible. Do the same with the other eye and make sure that they are positioned evenly. The eyes are now ready to be fastened in.

Pull each eye out far enough to see the loop or shank and place a drop of acrylic bonding glue in each hole. Pull the eyes back in and using a smaller needle take one cord from each eye under and out again about 6 mm/¼" from the original site. This will give you a base to knot your cords together. Pull each eye in firmly so that it sinks into the head a little and knot it securely. One at a time, thread each cord underneath the head where it can be cut close to the fabric. Pull the knot under as you do it; this will sink the knot and hide the ends.

The head will now have securely attached eyes with no knots showing and no loose threads.

The nose: Trim the fur back closely in a small triangle around the tip of the nose where the joining seams form a T. Experiment with the size and shape of nose you want with a template made from scrap paw felt or leather. When you have the shape you want, glue the template into place with the acrylic glue.

Choose the colour of thread (DMC Nos. 3 or 5) you want for the nose and use a fairly long sharp needle. Double the thread for the larger bears in Patterns Two and Three, but keep it single for the Pattern One bear. — the whole muzzle, back to the eyes and cheeks.

Start by passing the thread back and forth behind the template several times to secure it and then carefully stitch the nose in whichever style you prefer (Fig 10). When you have finished the mouth, take the thread down to the base of the neck joint and sink the knot.

The secret of stitching a good nose is to take your time, keep your tension fairly tight and even, and to keep your stitches very close together.

Trimming the nose: Your bear's character can be changed dramatically depending on how you wish to trim his nose and face. He can be left shaggy or shaved down to the fabric, or trimmed to any degree between these two extremes.

It is easy to be frightened of making a mistake in trimming fur, but with a little practice you should find it one of the most satisfying parts of bear-making.

Use small pointed scissors and make sure that they are sharp. The main thing to remember is to cut in the direction of the fur for a natural effect. This is usually from the tip of the nose back towards the head, so always cut with the tips of the scissors pointing towards the head. If you cut across the nap of the fur it is the same as if you cut across you own fringe or bangs. You will be left with a straight line. On your own head it can be desirable but on a bear it does not look very natural.

You can achieve a variety of looks by trimming:
— only the top of the nose, back to the forehead
— only the chin, under the mouth line and back to the neck
— the top of the nose and the chin
— the whole muzzle, back to the eyes and cheeks.

Practise and see what look you like in a bear. You will also find that different furs, for example, distressed, wavy or tipped mohair, look better cut in different ways.

Fig 10 — Nose stitching, some styles

The ears: Thread your needle with the dangling thread from the ear, turn the open edges under and sew them together with small stitches. Position the ears on the head and pin into place. Move them around until you are happy with them, using the head seams as guidelines to keep them level.

The ears look best if they are nicely curved and lifelike. In order to position them so, first pin the top edge to the head seam, not quite halfway along the top of the head. Place a second pin about a third of the way along the ear, also along the head seam. Curve the rest of the ear down and pin it almost but not quite as far forward as the top edge.

Stitching on the ears can be difficult as it is done mostly by feel. With each stitch take a little of the base of the ear before dipping into the head then out at the other side. Keep the stitches close together and close to the base of the ear so that they do not show as you work from side to side. Knot at the base of the ear, then take the thread under and out a little way from the knot. Tug on the thread to sink the knot, then cut the thread close to the fabric.

Your head is now complete and the bear is ready to be jointed before the body is stuffed.

JOINTING

It is a good idea to joint the head to the body before putting on the limbs, in case the limb placements need adjusting from their original markings. Using a strong thread, sew a running stitch around the neck opening on the body about 6 mm/¼″ from the edge. Draw it in to allow a small opening for the screw and knot off.

Push the screw into the hole and on the inside place a hardboard disc, a washer (just the washer for the small bear) and the ordinary nut. Tighten until the head can just be moved, then superglue the nut onto the thread to secure it.

Alternatively, you can use a second nut tightened behind the first, giving the first nut a half turn in the opposite direction to help lock them together.

If you wish to use a lock nut on the neck, hold the base of the screw or bolt with a pair of fine-nosed pliers while tightening the lock nut with a spanner. When the nut touches the pliers, move the pliers to the end of the bolt and continue tightening until you cannot turn the nut anymore. Loosen it off with half a turn back and that should be the correct tightness. The main difficulty with using a lock nut on the neck joint is that if the pliers slip too much while you are trying to tighten the nut, you can strip the thread on the screw and ruin it.

Once the head is attached, the limbs can be jointed. Find the joint marks on the inside of each limb and, with an awl or knitting needle, poke a hole there large enough to take the bolt screws. On each screw, place a metal washer, followed by a hardboard disc if making the larger bears. Place this in each shoulder and hip, with the bolt pointing towards the body.

Make sure that the limb placements will look good before piercing the body, which is done using a needle through the markings inside the body as a guide. Make a bolt hole in the body with the awl or knitting needle and push the appropriate limb's bolt through it into the body. On the inside of the body, place a hardboard disc, a washer (just the washer for the small bear) and a nyloc lock nut. The nylon ring inside the nut should show at the top.

Holding the bolt end inside the limb with a pair of pliers or a spanner, tighten the nut end inside the body with another spanner or adjustable wrench. Tighten it all the way and then loosen it back half a turn. Test the joint by trying to move it. You should just be able to move it, as it will move more easily when the limb is stuffed and acts as a lever. It is better to have the joint a little stiffer than you expect it to be in the finished bear. If the limb swings too freely before the bear is stuffed it will be too loose to hold a pose once he is finished.

STUFFING THE LIMBS AND THE BODY

Your very thin bear now has strong secure joints and is ready to be stuffed. Again, remember to start with firmly packed paw tips and work up the limb, feeling for gaps and lumps. When you are satisfied that each limb is well stuffed, with no stuffing protruding from the opening, the final seams are ready to be closed.

Refer to Fig 9 for the details on ladder stitch, which is used for closing all seams. Start at the top of the hole, using the last visible stitch as a marker for your first stitch. Pull your stitches together and tuck the edges in as you go. Finish with a knot in the seam, below the previous stitching, and pull it under to sink it.

When stuffing the body, be sure to pack firmly around the neck and shoulders so that the head does not wobble. Also pack firmly around the hips and bottom so that the bear will sit properly.

If you are using a growler, squeaker or music box, now is the time to position it and pack around it.

If you are aiming for a firmly stuffed bear it is a good idea to double your thread for the closing seams. It can be very frustrating to snap a thread in the middle of finishing a seam.

Claws, embroidered with the same thread used for the nose, can be put on if desired. Most teddy bears seem to have four claws, although real bears have five. A single thread will do for pattern number one, double thread for the larger bears.

Your bear is now finished and ready for a ribbon. Make sure that you check every seam for caught fur and give him a gentle brushing. Check that all his joints move freely and that any mechanisms you might have placed in him are functioning properly. If you have encountered any problems in making your bear the next chapter should be of some assistance.

CHAPTER 9

PROBLEM AREAS

There are always problem areas for any beginner, and learning to make bears is no exception. In many cases it is just a process of acquiring new skills and you will find that things become easier with each bear that you make.

SEAMS

If you are using long or thick fur, you may have difficulty in sewing the seams. Make sure that all the fur is pushed inside before you pin the edges together. As mentioned before, if the seam edge is especially curved, or the fur very thick, it will help if you overcast the seam then turn it right side out and tease out the fur from the seam edge. Turn it back inside out and sew the seam. You will find that the edges will lie flatter, be easier to sew and when you turn out the piece there will hardly be any fur caught in the seam.

When you turn your pieces, always ease out any caught fur from the seams with a needle. If you leave it until the bear is finished you might forget, an oversight that can detract from his appeal, or by that time the caught fur can be permanently crushed and does not flow with the rest of the fur.

If you sew your seams too close to the edge, they may rip out when you turn or stuff your bear. This can also happen if you machine sew the seams using too tight a tension on the thread. Always allow a minimum of a 6 mm/¼″ seam edge, even on a small bear, and remember to run glue along any seam openings before you turn. If you do rip out a seam, remove the stitches and turn the section inside out. Use the PVA glue along the edge, about 6 mm/¼″ wide along the frayed section. Let it dry and then try stitching the seam again over the glued edge. This should give a firm enough border to work on and enable the piece to be salvaged.

EYE AND JOINT PLACEMENT

As already outlined, it is a good idea to place your eyes in position before finally gluing and pulling them into place. If you decide that they are not even or badly positioned and you want to make another hole this is not necessarily a problem.

Providing that:

a) you used an awl or a knitting needle and did not rip a hole in the fabric,

b) the eye will still cover the wrongly placed hole from the new position, and

c) you have not already glued the eye into place,

you should have another chance.

Take the eye out and tease the fabric together around the hole. A tiny drop of glue might help here. Make your new hole, thread in the eye, glue it and pull it back and knot it as previously detailed.

Joint repositioning is much the same. You will sometimes find that the original joint markings inside the body will be too high, giving the bear a hunched look. In order to drop the arms a little and give the bear a neck, the armholes will have to be repositioned a little lower.

Again, as long as the discs of the arm will still cover the orignal holes there is no problem. Simply remove the limb, tease the hole closed and darn it from the inside. Make your new hole and joint the bear as before.

The same procedure applies for legs that are too low and close together or too wide and high.

EAR RE-PLACEMENT

You may be satisfied with the pinned on ears but find that after you have sewn on one it looks lower than the merely pinned on ear. This is only because the stitching has pulled it in closer to the head. You should find that the other ear should match it once it is also sewn on.

If you are dissatisfied with the ears after they are sewn on, they can easily be removed and re-sewn without leaving any marks. Just pull the ear back to expose a stitch and snip it to unravel your stitching.

PAW PAD SHAPE

Paws can be easily distorted by clumsy sewing or hasty machining, as well as by poor stuffing. This is best avoided by sewing and stuffing carefully and methodically.

NOSE STITCHING

As with everything, here practice makes perfect. If you are not happy with your embroidery, cut through the nose threads, pull out the ends with pliers and start again. It is easier to get a smooth even nose with one layer of stitches over a template than to sew another layer on top of an uneven layer.

Remember to keep your tension even and tight and to untwist your threads as you go if you are using a double thread.

You may find that the fur around the nose pulls into your stitches. A good way to avoid this is to stick the fur down away from the muzzle with 'magic' or removeable sticky tape.

LOOSE JOINTS

If you are using the nyloc nut system outlined in this book you will find that your joints are secure and will last indefinitely without slipping. You may, however, have not tightened the joints enough before stuffing and find that after stuffing they are too loose.

Unfortunately the only way to rectify this is to remove the stuffing from both sides of the joint and to tighten it with the two spanners. It is always best to err on the tight side rather than the loose side when jointing a bear.

CHAPTER 10

FINAL DETAILS

One of the most enjoyable things about finishing a bear is to find just the right sort of adornment for him or her. You will find that every bear has a unique character, and your final touches should enhance it.

RIBBONS AND LACE

For some reason most bears seem to be male, and the really gruff ones only need a leather collar to bring out the beast in them. There is an endless range of ribbons to be found, both old and new, and it can be a pleasant task to find the right ribbon for the right bear.

For those few female bears, an antique lace collar can look charming. If you like dressing up your bears, you can have lots of fun with varying seasonal outfits.

SEWN-IN LABELS

If you are serious about your bear-making you should consider having a permanently attached label somewhere on each of your bears. These are usually small folded strips of ribbon, tape, suede or leather with the makers details either printed or hand-written on them. Both ends are sewn together onto one of the bear's seams, usually the back, side, or the rear of an arm or leg.

PERSONAL SYMBOLS

As well as an identifying label, many bear-makers use a personal symbol on their bears to make them unique. Some well-known symbols are a golden stud in one ear, a pewter button hanging around the neck, a studded collar, a heart stud on one wrist, embroidered paws, a grub rose in one ear and even a tail.

SWING TAGS

A final touch should be a swing tag giving the bear's details, date of birth, maker's name, etc. If the bear is an adult collectable and not a child's toy, be sure to mention it, even if it is just the line 'Not suitable for children'.

If you are seriously thinking of going into business for yourself, you can design your own logo. Remember to register your business name and your trademark or logo. You can use your logo on your business cards, letterheads, swing tags and labels.

A serious bear-maker will have a small fortune in fur and supplies on hand, so it will pay to look into the tax side of running a small business to see what deductions you are able to claim.

CHAPTER 11

REPAIR AND RESTORATION

This chapter is designed to give you some assistance in repairing love-worn old bears. If your bear is a potentially valuable antique, however, I would suggest taking him to an antique auction house for appraisal first. Any repairs or restoration work carried out on a rare old specimen must be of top quality or it may detract from, rather than add to, his value.

Whatever work needs to be done on your bear, the aim is to restore him to his original condition as closely as possible. This means that you must know what any missing parts originally looked like, something that may take a little research but will be well worthwhile in the end result.

If, for example, the bear's eyes are missing, his brand name and approximate age must be established so you can determine whether his eyes should be plastic, glass or possibly boot-buttons. It has been known for unscrupulous dealers to replace plastic or glass eyes with old boot-buttons in a recent bear in order to 'age' him and increase his value. Steiff buttons have also appeared in the ears of bears that are not Steiff; modern replica Steiff have been found to have been forcibly aged to pass as the older original version, and so on. It is unfortunate that these deceptions occur in the bear world, but luckily most can be spotted if you are careful and know your bears. These occurrences merely illustrate the fact that there is such worldwide interest in bears, and that your old bear could be quite valuable.

If you purchase an old bear to add to your collection, it is advisable to quarantine him first in order to remove any possible insect infestations. He can be sealed in a plastic bag for a few days with some mothballs, a 'bug bomb' or put into the freezer for 24 hours. When he is removed from the bag, gently shake him to dislodge any possible dead insects, then give him a brushing with a fine wire dog brush.

Occasional gentle vacuuming and brushing will remove surface dust and keep your bears in top form. Don't be too over-zealous with your grooming, though. I know of a lady who vacuumed and brushed her bear to complete baldness.

Providing that your old bear does not need surgery first, he can now be cleaned. Modern bears are often machine washable, or at least fully submersible, but if you are not sure, it is better to assume that he is not. This is especially true if he is excelsior stuffed.

Use a mild fabric detergent and dilute it, and also have a rinse bowl of clean water, sponges and cloths. Beat the detergent to suds and only use the froth, massaging them into the fur, but trying to keep the fabric backing or 'skin' dry. Rinse off with a clean damp cloth. Work on a small area at a time and repeat several times. Carefully towel dry and then air dry him out of direct sunlight, or dry him very gently with a hairdryer set on low and cool, finishing off with a brushing.

EYES

As previously mentioned, if your old bear needs new eyes, do some research to make sure that you will be giving him the right sort. If he is only missing one, you may find it easier to give him a pair of matched eyes rather than finding him an exact match for one old remaining eye. If he is completely blind, try several eye sizes before giving him sight, as the wrong sized eyes can really affect the whole appeal of the bear.

Sew them in with the same method as outlined in the step-by-step chapter (page 37), knotting the cords at the back of the neck disc and sinking the knot and the ends.

NOSE AND MOUTH

Match up the original thread as closely as possible. If there is no nose remaining, it may be necessary to research a little to find out the original nose shape, colour and direction of stitching. Again, follow the directions in Chapter 8 (page 37).

EARS

As ears are often the most common handles for small hands picking up loved bears, they are often abused or missing in old bears. If both ears are missing, new ones can be made from mohair or fabric that matches the bear as closely as possible. There are often marks on the head which indicate size and placement of the original ears, making it easier to replace them.

If there is still one ear left and the fabric is difficult to match, you may find it easier to carefully remove and dismantle the remaining ear, cut out another in as close a match as possible, and make up two ears, each with one old side and one new side. They can then be sewn on with the original fur showing on each ear lining and the new fur on each ear back for an even look.

PAW PADS

Old felt paw pads often wear thin or have bad moth holes. If they are not too bad they should be left alone, but if the stuffing is coming out the pads should be repaired.

Felt can be dyed to match existing pads, often by merely soaking it in cold tea or coffee for a subtle shading. If the pads are made of rexine, a type of oil-cloth, they can be reproduced by painting cotton cloth with a matching brown paint. When dry, crumple the fabric to reproduce the cracks usually found on rexine pads. Leather or suede pads can be matched with scraps brought from craft or leather shops.

The new paw pad is cut to shape and neatly oversewn into place with tiny stitches. If using felt, it can be gently shaped and stretched over a steaming kettle prior to sewing.

PATCHING HOLES

Before repairing any holes, split seams, rips, etc. it is a good idea to use the diluted PVA glue on all the exposed fabric edges and let them dry. This wil give you an invisible yet strong seam edge to sew over, and prevent your stitches from tearing out.

If you need to patch an area, push a piece of matching fabric underneath the edges of the hole and sew around the edge with ladder stitch. Old fabric can be very fragile so be careful when sewing up an old bear. Often small holes are better glued to prevent further fraying instead of being darned over.

Missing limbs can be replaced by measuring existing ones, drawing patterns for them and making them from matching fabric. To re-attach them you will have to open up the body along its original closing seam, in order to reach both sides of the joint.

STUFFING

In old bears, especially those that are excelsior stuffed, the stuffing often settles or even breaks down, leaving bears looking very droopy and empty. While this does give an old bear a lot of character, there are instances when a little re-stuffing can do a lot to revitalise a bear. This is very true when the stuffing has been lost from the shoulders, neck and hump.

If your bear needs a little re-stuffing, find his original closing seams and carefully open him there. On the body it may be at either the front or the back; on the limbs it may be at the front, the back or even on the top curve. Match up his stuffing, and if you are using wood-wool or excelsior, cut it into manageable lengths first. Restuff the empty areas carefully, keeping in mind that his overall feel should not be changed, and close him up with ladder stitch. If working on his body, this is a good time to check if he has a growler, squeaker or music box inside him. If it is not working you may wish to replace it. The condition of his joints can also be examined.

RE-TUFTING

Until recently, if your prized bear had bald spots there was nothing that could be done. Now there are specialists available who can re-tuft your bare bear with colours hand-mixed to perfectly match his mohair. This is a labourious process, rather like making a hooked rug, and can add several thousands of dollars to the cost of your bear. If it is done on a rare specimen and restores him to his original splendour, however, it can also add thousands to his value.

CARE AND MAINTENANCE

Finally, your precious collection should be looked after well. Always keep your bears out of direct sunlight, which will fade colours and make the fur brittle, and keep them free of dust, which can attract moths, as well as keeping them away from damp. If they are packed away, be careful of pressure spots, crushed ears, metal pins, tight bands, etc. In tropical climates insects can be a real problem, and if you cannot afford glass cabinets for your collection, try keeping cedar blocks or bowls of camphor amongst them.

CHAPTER 12

A FINAL NOTE

I hope that you have found this book interesting and informative, and have discovered for yourself the joys of making teddy bears. As the saying goes — try stopping at one! As soon as you have made your first bear, you will find yourself besieged with requests from your children, your friends and your relations.

I made my first bear just to see if it could be done and I intended to keep it. Now, after several years of making bears and constantly evolving my designs, I have yet to make one that I get to keep. Apart from an ever-increasing waiting list, a bear-collecting friend is getting married and I know just what she needs for a wedding present, my new nephew must have a bear for his first Christmas ... and one day I'll make a bear just for myself.

TEDDY BEAR ASSOCIATIONS

THE ANTIPODEAN BEAR MAKERS CO-OP

PO Box 274
Concord NSW 2137
Australia

IN TEDDIES WE TRUST

PO Box 297
Rosebery NSW 2018
Australia

THE TEDDY BEAR ARTISTS ASSOCIATION

PO Box 905
Woodland Hills
CA 91365
USA

GOOD BEARS OF THE WORLD
INTERNATIONAL

2352 Valeway Drive
Toledo Ohio 43613
USA

BRITISH TEDDY BEAR ASSOCIATION

Hugglets
PO Box 290
Brighton BN2 1DR
UK

SUPPLY DIRECTORY

There are naturally many more suppliers than the ones listed, but these will give you a good idea of the range available. The American suppliers generally have German mohair, while the English ones usually stock English mohair.

CERAMIC SUPPLY CENTRE

52 Wecker Road
Mansfield, Brisbane
QLD 4122
Australia

BUMBLEWOOD

52 Bevendean Avenue
Saltdean, E. Sussex
BN28PF
UK

EDINBURGH IMPORTS INC.

PO Box 722
Woodland Hills
CA 91365-0722
USA

GERRY'S TEDDY & CRAFT DESIGNS

30 John Street
Rosewood
QLD 4340
Australia

BEAR ARTIST DIRECTORY

MARY FRANCES BALDO

MFB Enterprises
10702 Inwood Drive
Houston Texas 77042
USA

CAROL PEARCE

16126 La Avenida
Houston Texas 77062
USA

NATALIE & DANA BERGSTROM

37 King Street
Umina, NSW 2257

CAROL STEWART

903 NW Spruce Ridge Drive
Stuart Florida 34994
USA

GINGER T. BRAME

7405 Lake Tree Drive
Raleigh NC 27615
USA

BARBARA A. TROXEL

Bear Den Hollow
Rt 1 Box 48
Muscoda WI 53573
USA

DICKIE HARRISON

(not available)
USA

BILLEE HENDERSON

9312 Santayana Drive
Fairfax VA 22031
USA

BETH DIANE HOGAN

5629 N Bonfair Avenue
Lakewood CA 90712
USA

JENNIFER LAING

6 Walter Road
Ingleside NSW 2101
Australia

CINDY LOWE

PO Box 274
Concord NSW 2137
Australia

KAY VANDERLEY

26 Bissett Street
Kempsey NSW 2440
Australia

JUDY & MICHAEL WALTON

Akatarawa Road
RD 2 Upper Hutt
New Zealand

GERRY WARLOW

30 John Street
Rosewood QLD 4340
Australia

BONNIE WINDELL

6611 Red Horse Pike
Newburgh IN 47630
USA

R. JOHN WRIGHT

15 West Main Street
Cambridge NY 12816
USA

BOOKBINDER

Luxury bindings in leather and gold, limited editions and one-of-a-kind books, repair and restoration. Commissions taken.

TERRY COLLINS

P.O. Box 365
Rozelle NSW 2039
Australia

MUSEUMS AND SHOPS

There are too many toy museums and bear shops around the world to mention, but here are some of my favourites.

MUSEUMS

THE STEIFF MUSEUM

Margaret Steiff GmbH
PO Box 1560, Alliin Strasse 2
Giengen (Brenz) D-7928
Germany

FRANNIE'S TEDDY BEAR MUSEUM

2511 Pine Ridge Road
Naples, FL 33942
USA

**BETHNAL GREEN MUSEUM
OF CHILDHOOD**

Cambridge Heath Road
London E29PA
UK

SHOPS

THE TEDDY BEAR SHOP

162 Military Road
Neutral Bay, NSW 2089
Australia

TEDDIES

1961 Route 33
Hamilton Square, NJ 08690
USA

TEDDY BEARS

99 High Street, Witney
Oxfordshire OX8 6LY
UK

PAM HEBBS

5 The Annexe, Camden Passage
Islington, London N1
UK

LIST OF PLATES

COVER

Bears by Jennifer Laing, handbound set of 'Winnie the Pooh' books by Terry Collins, embroidered picture and cushions by Jennifer Laing, lamp and tablecloth from Stratton's of Mosman.

PLATE 1

Vintage Steiffs from 1904-1910. Large bears from the collection of David Worland, small bear from Julie Townsend's collection, bear on wheels from the author's collection.

PLATE 2

An early English Farnell with an early Steiff, courtesy of David Worland. The Farnell is very similar to the original Winnie the Pooh, the Stieff a rare centre-seam bear.

PLATE 3

Profile of an early Steiff, displaying the classic teddy bear proportions and character.

PLATE 4

Modern limited edition replicas of old Steiff bears.
Back row, left to right: sitting white muzzle bear (without his muzzle on), 1990; standing cream bear produced for the UK only, 1992; standing gold Giengen Mama (without baby), 1984.
Middle row: (sitting on bear on wheels) small white Dicky from Circus set, 1990; sitting gold Dicky, 1985; Mr Cinnamon musical, produced for Harrods, 1990; small cinnamon Margaret Strong bear with leather paws, 1984.
Front row: sitting white Snap-Apart, 1991; bear on wheels, 1985; small gold Dicky bear from Circus set, 1990; gold bear from Nimrod set (undressed), 1983; baby Jackie, 1989.

PLATE 5

Accessories. An assortment of miniature accoutrements for bears found at various antique markets around the world.

PLATE 6

Artist Bears — 12″–16″ (30 cm–4 cm).
Left: sitting black bear by Billee Henderson. Back: gold bear by Kay Van Derley.
Centre: silver-tipped pellet-filled bear by Jennifer Laing.
Right: gold bent-leg pellet-filled bear by Carol Pearce.

PLATE 7

Artist Bears — 6″–12″ (15 cm–30 cm). *Back left*: honey bear by Judy and Michael Walton.
Centre, on chair: Winnie the Pooh by R John Wright.
Back right: Tessa by Jennifer Laing
Front, from left: sitting ginger bear by Cindy Lowe; bear with sweater by Ginger Brame; brown bear by Bonnie Windell and grey-tipped bear by Barbara Troxel.

PLATE 8

Miniature bears — 4″ (10 cm) and under. Golden bear on rocking horse by Natalie and Dana Bergstrom; bear with balloon by Mary Frances Baldo.
Far right: standing gold mini Steiff bear from the 1950s, and sitting in front of him a gold mini Schuco bear from the 1940s.
Far left: standing Schuco panda from the 1950s, and sitting in front of him a smaller Schuco panda from the 1940s. Bear on wheels by Beth Diane Hogan; to his right, gold bear with red collar by Dickie Harrison; jester bear by Gerry Warlow; Winnie the Pooh and sailor bear both by Carol Stewart; brown bent-leg bear by Beth Diane Hogan; and tiny bear with lace collar by Jennifer Laing.

PLATE 9

Materials and Tools. A selection of mohair at the back and felt at the front. Polyfill stuffing on the right and some plastic pellets on the felt. Nose threads and sewing threads on the left with long eye needles in front, next to glass eyes and boot-buttons. Jointing tools with joint hardware and discs. At the back is an awl and a pair of needle-nosed pliers, while at the front are some small scissors and a wire finishing brush.

PLATE 10

Pattern Bears. On the left is Pattern Three, a large bent-arm-and-leg bear. On the right is Pattern Two, a medium sized old-fashioned bear, and in front is Pattern One, a small beginner's bear.

PLATE 11

Pattern One bear.

PLATE 12

Pattern Two bear.

PLATE 13

Pattern Three bear.

BIBLIOGRAPHY

ANTIQUE AND MODERN TEDDY BEARS

Kim Brewer & Carol-Lynn Rossel Waugh, House of Collectibles, New York, USA, 1990

THE ULTIMATE TEDDY BEAR BOOK

Pauline Cockrill, Dorling Kindersley, New York, USA, 1991

COLLECTING TEDDY BEARS

Pam Hebbs, William Collins Sons & Co, London, UK, 1988

TEDDY BEARS PAST AND PRESENT

Linda Mullins, Hobby House Press, Maryland, USA, 1986

THE TEDDY BEAR LOVERS CATALOG

Ted Menton, Courage Books, PA, USA, 1983

TEDDY BEAR ARTIST'S ANNUAL — WHO'S WHO IN BEAR MAKING

Rosemary & Paul Volpp, Donna Harrison and Dottie Ayres, Hobby House Press, Maryland, USA, 1989

STEIFF-SENSATIONAL TEDDY BEARS, ANIMALS AND DOLLS

Rolf & Christel Pistorius, Hobby House Press, Maryland, USA, 1990

MAGAZINES

BEAR FACTS REVIEW

PO Box 680, Goulburn, NSW 2580, Australia

TEDDY BEAR AND FRIENDS

Hobby House Press, 900 Frederick Street, Cumberland, MA 21502, USA

TEDDY BEAR REVIEW

Collector Communications Corp., PO Box 1239, Hanover, PA 17331, USA

HUGGLETS TEDDY BEAR MAGAZINE

PO Box 290, Brighton BN2 1DR, UK

TEDDY BEAR TIMES

Ashdown Publishing, Shelley House, 104 High Street, Steyning, W. Sussex BN4 3RD, UK